Cute Skull

COLORING BOOK

RELAXATION AND MINDFULNESS

SURPRISE!

Hi!

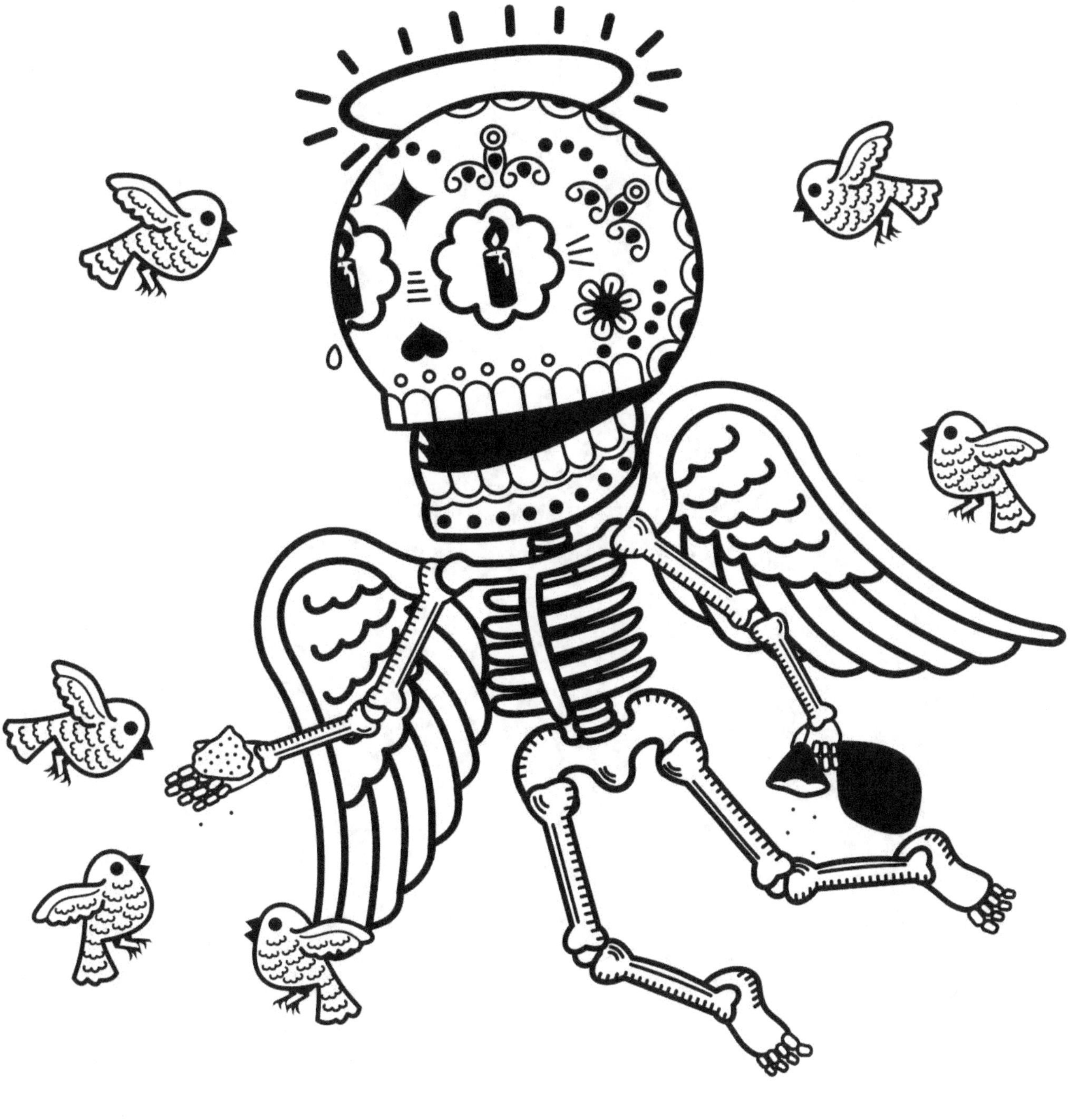

I'M FINE

Yuck!!!

FALLEN ANGEL

Bingo!

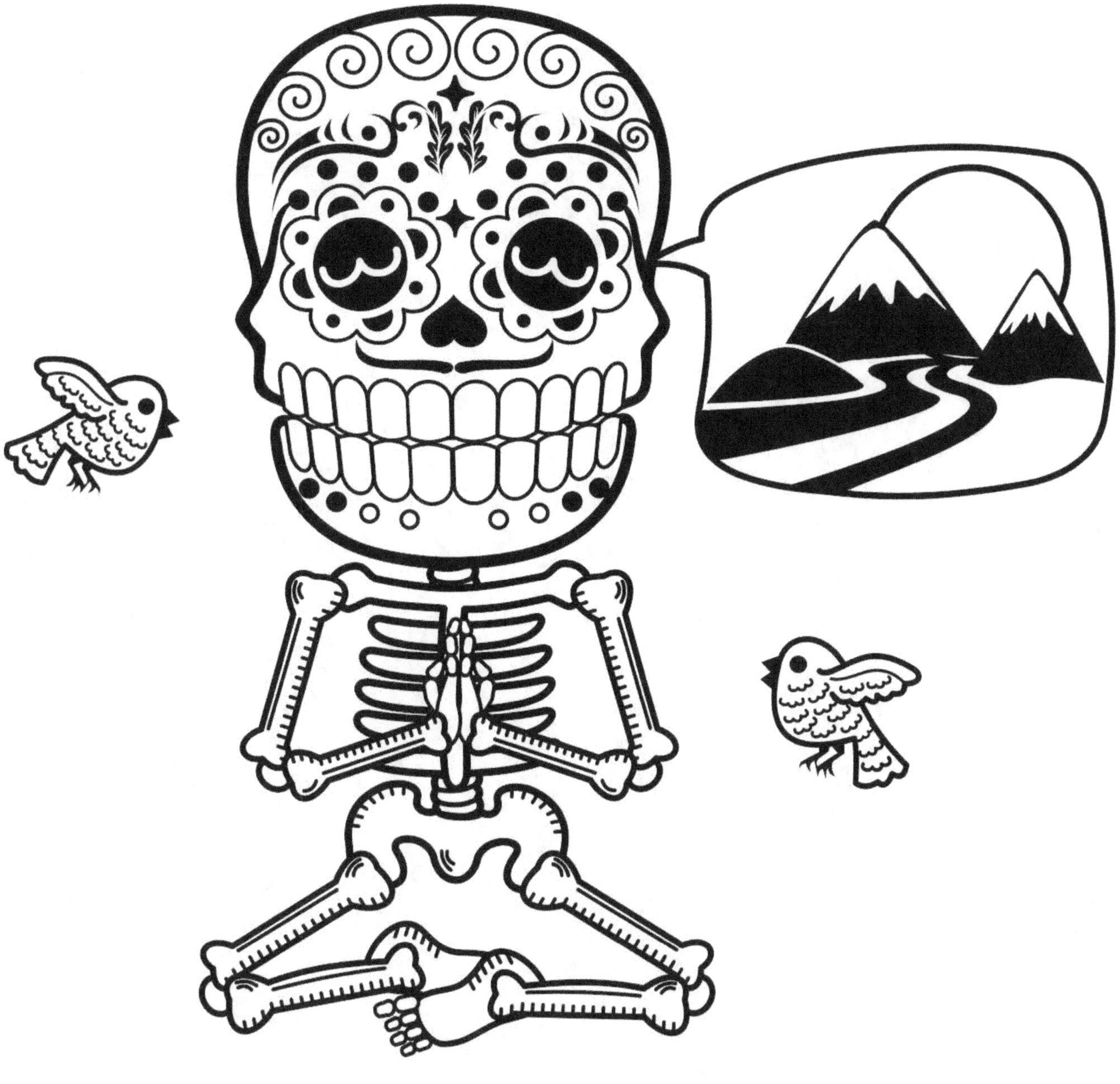

WOW!

MEMENTO MORI

DRY UP!

Victory!

www.ingramcontent.com/pod-product-compliance
Lightning Source LLC
Chambersburg PA
CBHW081154280526
45787CB00008B/3327
9781548043698